Tower Air Fryer Cookbook UK 2023

800 Days Flavorful and Healthy Air Fryer Recipes with British Measurements & Ingredients for Hassle-Free Frying and Cooking.

By Corina Musat

CONTENTS

INTRODUCTION

What is an Air Fryer and what does it do?

A modern kitchen appliance called an air fryer cooks food without the need of oil by circulating hot air over it. It offers low-fat variations of foods that are frequently deep-fried. As a result, conventionally harmful foods like fried chicken, onion rings, and French fries are made with up to 80% less fat than they would otherwise. The Air Fryer provides healthier alternatives of fried foods and meals that still have the required crisp, texture, and quality while saving you from the calories associated with frying.

A food item is placed in an enclosed space, and this home appliance quickly and uniformly circulates extremely hot air (up to 250°C) around it. The food component becomes crisp and dry on the outside and soft and moist within as a result of the heat. An air fryer can be used to cook almost anything. In addition to frying, you can also roast, bake, and grill. Since there are so many different ways to cook, it is easier to create any type of meal at any time of day.

Why Do You Need An Air Fryer?

Low-Fat Meals: The air fryer's greatest benefit is without a doubt the use of hot air circulation to cook food ingredients from all sides without the need of oil. Now it's simple for people on a low-fat diet to make scrumptious meals.

Healthier Foods: Since air fryers don't utilize bad oils, they can produce food that is up to 80% less fatty while still being nutritious. This makes it easier to lose weight because you can still enjoy your favorite fried dishes while cutting back on the calories and saturated fat. This tool makes adopting a healthier lifestyle more feasible. Additionally, the scent of deep-fried food—which frequently lingers in the air for hours after deep-frying—is no longer present in your house.

Multipurpose Use: Several items can be cooked at simultaneously in an air fryer, allowing for multitasking. Your preferred cuisine can be grilled, baked, fried, or roasted using this multipurpose utensil! You no longer need numerous appliances for various jobs. It is capable of more jobs than separate appliances. It can grill meat, roast veggies, and bake pastries. In place of your stovetop, oven, and deep fryer, it works well.

Extremely Safe: Bear in mind that adding chicken or other foods to the deep fryer requires extra caution. You want to make sure that it doesn't spill and burn your flesh because it is constantly quite hot. If you utilized an air fryer, you wouldn't have to worry about burning flesh due to hot oil leaking. It handles all the frying and is completely safe. Wearing cooking gloves, however, will protect you from heat hazards while moving your fryer. Keep children away from your air fryer, too.

Save Time: People with busy schedules can quickly create delicious meals with the air fryer's quickness. For instance, it takes 25 minutes to bake a cake and less than 15 minutes to make French fries. In a matter of minutes, you can also eat crispy chicken tenders or golden fries. You will spend less time in the kitchen if you use the air fryer if you are always on the go. It helps you manage your busy daily routine and makes your day less stressful.

Easy Clean-Up: The Air Fryer leaves no grease behind, thus no mess is created. Cleaning time is enjoyable because there are no plans to scrape or scrub and no oil spills to clean up on the walls or floors. It is needless to spend time making sure everything is immaculate. The Air fryer components' non-stick coating prevents food from sticking to surfaces, making cleanup more challenging. These parts are easy to clean and maintain. They are also removable and dishwasher-safe.

Important Tips for using Air Fryer Efficiently

Keep It Dry: Before cooking, pat meals, particularly those that have been marinated, dry. More smoke and splattering will be reduced by doing this. Foods containing a lot of fat, like chicken breast and wings, usually release fat when they are cooked. Therefore, take care to regularly drain the accumulated fat from the air fryer's bottom.

Space Your Foods: The ideal practice when using an air fryer is to avoid congestion. If you want your food to cook correctly, give it adequate room so that air can move about. Right, you want to enjoy how crispy your meal is. The close quarters prevent the food from breathing. Therefore, be sure to space out your meals.

Shake the Foods: After the food has been cooking for a few minutes, open the Air Fryer and shake the items within. Chips, French fries, and other small foods can be shaken around to prevent compression. Rotate food every five to ten minutes to ensure optimal cooking and formation.

Spray Your Food: You'll need cooking spray when using your air fryer since it prevents food from sticking to the basket. Foods can either be lightly sprayed with oil or simply added.

Batch Cooking: The air fryer has a constrained cooking capacity. If you are cooking for a large gathering, you must prepare the meal in batches.

Preheat: Pre-heat the air fryer if it hasn't been used for a while. Pre-heat it for three to five minutes to ensure proper heating.

BREAKFAST RECIPES

Breakfast Turkey Burrito

Prep Time: 10 Min | Cook Time: 10 Min | Serves: 2

Calories: 348.8 | Fat: 23.0g | Carbs: 22.1g | Protein: 19.8g

INGREDIENTS

- 4 slices turkey breast already cooked
- ½ red bell pepper, sliced
- 2 eggs
- 1 small avocado, peeled, pitted and sliced
- 2 tbsp salsa
- Salt and black pepper to the taste
- 30g mozzarella cheese, grated
- Tortillas for serving

DIRECTIONS

1. Eggs should be beaten with salt and pepper to taste in a bowl before being poured into a pan and placed in the air fryer's basket.
2. After five minutes of cooking at 200°C, remove the pan from the fryer and place the eggs on a plate.
3. Place tortillas in a row on a work surface. Distribute eggs, turkey meat, bell pepper, cheese, salsa, and avocado among them.
4. After lining your air fryer with some tin foil, roll your burritos and put them inside.
5. The burritos should be heated for 3 minutes at 150°C, then divided among plates.

Polenta Bites

Prep Time: 10 Min | Cook Time: 20 Min | Serves: 4

Calories: 230.9 | Fat: 6.9g | Carbs: 11.3g | Protein: 3.6g

INGREDIENTS

For the polenta:

- 1 tbsp butter
- 250g cornmeal
- 750ml water
- Salt and black pepper to the taste

For the polenta bites:

- 2 tbsp powdered sugar
- Cooking spray

DIRECTIONS

1. Cornmeal, water, butter, salt, and pepper should be combined in a skillet and cooked for 10 minutes before being removed from the heat and kept in the refrigerator to cool.

2. Scoop out one spoonful of polenta, roll it into a ball, and set it on the work surface.

3. Repeat with the remaining polenta, place all the balls in your air fryer's cooking basket, coat them with cooking spray, cover the pan, and cook for 8 minutes at 195°C.

4. To serve polenta bites for breakfast, arrange them on plates and sprinkle with sugar.

Sweet Breakfast Casserole

Prep Time: 10 Min | Cook Time: 25 Min | Serves: 4

Calories: 213.4 | Fat: 5.0g | Carbs: 12.1g | Protein: 5.1g

INGREDIENTS

- 3 tbsp brown sugar
- 4 tbsp butter
- 2 tbsp white sugar
- ½ tsp cinnamon powder
- 125g flour

For the casserole:

- 2 eggs
- 2 tbsp white sugar

- 650g white flour
- 1 tsp baking soda
- 1 tsp baking powder
- 2 eggs
- 125ml milk
- 450ml buttermilk
- 4 tbsp butter
- Zest from 1 lemon, grated
- 350g blueberries

DIRECTIONS

1. Eggs should be combined with 2 tbsp of white sugar, white flour, baking powder, baking soda, 2 eggs, milk, buttermilk, 4 tbsp of butter, lemon zest, and blueberries in a dish. The mixture should then be stirred and poured into an air fryer-compatible pan.

2. Spread the crumble over the blueberries mixture by combining 3 tbsp brown sugar, 2 tbsp white sugar, 4 tbsp butter, and 125g flour in another bowl.

3. Place in an air fryer that has been preheated and bake for 30 minutes at 150°C.

4. For breakfast, divide among plates. Serve and enjoy!

Sausage, Eggs and Cheese Mix

Prep Time: 10 Min | Cook Time: 20 Min | Serves: 4

Calories: 318.6 | Fat: 6.0g | Carbs: 12.1g | Protein: 4.9g

INGREDIENTS

- 300g sausages, cooked and crumbled
- 250g cheddar cheese, shredded
- 250g mozzarella cheese, shredded
- 8 eggs, whisked
- 250ml milk
- Salt and black pepper to the taste
- Cooking spray

DIRECTIONS

1. Sausage, mozzarella, cheese, eggs, milk, salt, and pepper should all be combined with a whisk in a bowl.

2. Spray frying oil in your air fryer, preheat to 195°Cahrenheit, add the eggs and sausage mixture, and cook for 20 minutes.

3. Serve and enjoy!

Cheese Bake

Prep Time: 10 Min | Cook Time: 20 Min | Serves: 4

Calories: 213.6 | Fat: 5.0g | Carbs: 12.1g | Protein: 11.9g

INGREDIENTS

- 4 bacon slices, cooked and crumbled
- 500ml milk
- 250g cheddar cheese, shredded
- ½ kg breakfast sausage, casings removed and chopped
- 2 eggs
- ½ tsp onion powder
- Salt and black pepper to the taste
- 3 tbsp parsley, chopped
- Cooking spray

DIRECTIONS

1. Whisk the eggs, milk, cheese, onion powder, salt, pepper, and parsley together in a bowl.
2. Add bacon and sausage to your air fryer after greasing it with cooking spray and heating it to 160°C.
3. For 20 minutes, spread the egg mixture and add it.
4. Serve and enjoy!

Tofu Scramble

Prep Time: 5 Min | Cook Time: 30 Min | Serves: 4

Calories: 139.8 | Fat: 4.0g | Carbs: 10.1g | Protein: 13.8g

INGREDIENTS

- 2 tbsp soy sauce
- 1 tofu block, cubed
- 1 tsp turmeric, ground
- 2 tbsp extra virgin olive oil
- 750g broccoli florets
- ½ tsp onion powder
- ½ tsp garlic powder
- 500g red potatoes, cubed
- 125g yellow onion, chopped
- Salt and black pepper to the taste

DIRECTIONS

1. In a bowl, combine the tofu, 1 tbsp of oil, salt, pepper, soy sauce, garlic powder, onion powder, turmeric, and onion. Stir to combine, then set aside.
2. Combine potatoes with the remaining oil, a dash of salt, and some pepper in a separate bowl, and toss to coat.
3. Bake potatoes in your air fryer for 15 minutes, shaking the pan once, at 175°C.
4. In your air fryer, add the tofu and bake for 15 minutes.
5. Fry the broccoli with the other ingredients for an additional five minutes.

Oatmeal Casserole

Prep Time: 10 Min | Cook Time: 20 Min | Serves: 8

Calories: 299.8 | Fat: 4.1g | Carbs: 12.2g | Protein: 9.6g

INGREDIENTS

- 450g rolled oats
- 1 tsp baking powder
- 45g brown sugar
- 1 tsp cinnamon powder
- 125g chocolate chips
- 150g blueberries
- 1 banana, peeled and mashed
- 500ml milk
- 1 eggs
- 2 tbsp butter
- 1 tsp vanilla extract
- Cooking spray

DIRECTIONS

1. Banana, blueberries, chocolate chips, cinnamon, baking powder, and sugar are combined in a bowl and stirred.
2. Butter, vanilla extract, and eggs should be combined and stirred in a separate bowl.
3. As soon as your air fryer reaches 160°Cahrenheit, oil the bottom with cooking spray and add the oats.
4. Stir in the egg mixture and cinnamon mixture, then bake for 20 minutes.
5. Then divide the mixture into bowls and serve as breakfast.

Ham Breakfast

Prep Time: 10 Min | Cook Time: 15 Min | Serves: 6

Calories: 199.7 | Fat: 4.8g | Carbs: 12.1g | Protein: 13.6g

INGREDIENTS

- 750g French bread, cubed
- 100g green chilies, chopped
- 300g ham, cubed
- 100g cheddar cheese, shredded
- 500ml milk
- 5 eggs
- 1 tbsp mustard
- Salt and black pepper to the taste
- Cooking spray

DIRECTIONS

1. Cooking spray should be used to oil and pre-heat your air fryer to 175°C.
2. Mix the eggs, milk, cheese, mustard, salt, and pepper in a bowl.
3. In your air fryer, combine bread cubes, ham, and chilies.
4. For 15 minutes, spread the egg mixture and add it.
5. Serve and enjoy!

Tomato and Bacon Breakfast

Prep Time: 10 Min | Cook Time: 30 Min | Serves: 6

Calories: 230.4 | Fat: 4.9g | Carbs: 12.1g | Protein: 4.2g

INGREDIENTS

- ½ kg white bread, cubed
- ½ kg smoked bacon, cooked and chopped
- 50ml olive oil
- 1 yellow onion, chopped
- 750g canned tomatoes, chopped
- ½ tsp red pepper, crushed
- ¼ kg cheddar, shredded
- 2 tbsp chives, chopped
- ¼ kg Monterey jack, shredded
- 2 tbsp stock
- Salt and black pepper to the taste
- 8 eggs, whisked

DIRECTIONS

1. Your air fryer should be heated to 175°C after adding the oil.
2. Stir in the stock, bread, bacon, onion, tomatoes, and red pepper.
3. Add eggs, cheddar and Monterey jack and cook everything for 20 minutes.
4. Place a portion on each plate, top with chives, and serve.

Blackberry French Toast

Prep Time: 10 Min | Cook Time: 30 Min | Serves: 6

Calories: 214.5 | Fat: 5.9g | Carbs: 15.1g | Protein: 6.2g

INGREDIENTS

- 250ml blackberry jam, warm
- 350g bread loaf, cubed
- 225g cream cheese, cubed
- 4 eggs
- 1 tsp cinnamon powder
- 65g brown sugar
- 1 tsp vanilla extract
- Cooking spray

DIRECTIONS

1. Use cooking spray to grease your air fryer and heat it to 150°C.
2. Layer half of the bread cubes, blueberry jam, cream cheese, and remaining bread on top of the first layer.
3. In a bowl, mix eggs with half and half, cinnamon, sugar and vanilla, whisk well and add over bread mix.
4. Cook for 20 minutes, divide among plates and serve for breakfast.

Smoked Sausage Breakfast Mix

Prep Time: 10 Min | Cook Time: 30 Min | Serves: 4

Calories: 319.6 | Fat: 5.9g | Carbs: 17.1g | Protein: 4.2g

INGREDIENTS

- 750g smoked sausage, chopped and browned
- A pinch of salt and black pepper
- 400g grits
- 1000ml water
- 450g cheddar cheese, shredded
- 250ml milk
- ¼ tsp garlic powder
- 1 and ½ tsp thyme, chopped
- Cooking spray
- 4 eggs, whisked

DIRECTIONS

1. Add the grits to the boiling water in a pot over medium heat, stir, cover, and cook for 5 minutes before turning off the heat.
2. Add the cheese, swirl until it melts, then whisk in the milk, thyme, salt, pepper, garlic powder, and eggs.
3. Heat up your air fryer at 150°C, grease with cooking spray and add browned sausage.
4. Add grits mix, spread and cook for 25 minutes.
5. Serve and enjoy!

Quick Spicy Potatoes

Prep Time: 10 Min | Cook Time: 35 Min | Serves: 4

Calories: 213.8 | Fat: 6.1g | Carbs: 14.3g | Protein: 4.2g

INGREDIENTS

- 2 tbsp olive oil
- 3 potatoes, cubed
- 1 yellow onion, chopped
- 1 red bell pepper, chopped
- Salt and black pepper to the taste
- 1 tsp garlic powder
- 1 tsp sweet paprika
- 1 tsp onion powder

DIRECTIONS

1. Add potatoes to the oil-greased basket of the air fryer, mix, and season with salt and pepper.

2. Toss well, then add the onion, bell pepper, garlic powder, paprika, and onion powder. Cook, covered, at 185°C for 30 minutes.

3. Serve the potato mixture divided among plates as breakfast.

Corn Flakes Breakfast Casserole

Prep Time: 10 Min | Cook Time: 8 Min | Serves: 4

Calories: 297.4 | Fat: 5.0g | Carbs: 16.1g | Protein: 3.8g

INGREDIENTS

- 75ml milk
- 3 tsp sugar
- 2 eggs, whisked
- ¼ tsp nutmeg, ground
- 75g blueberries
- 4 tbsp cream cheese, whipped
- 250g corn flakes, crumbled
- 5 bread slices

DIRECTIONS

1. Whisk the eggs, milk, sugar, and nutmeg together in a bowl.
2. Blueberries and cream cheese should be thoroughly incorporated in a separate bowl.
3. In the third bowl, add corn flakes.
4. Each piece of bread should be spread with blueberry mixture, dipped in egg mixture, and then finished with corn flakes.
5. Place the bread in the basket of your air fryer, heat to 200°Cahrenheit, and bake for 8 minutes.
6. Serve and enjoy!

Ham Pie

Prep Time: 10 Min | Cook Time: 25 Min | Serves: 6

Calories: 397.5 | Fat: 26.3g | Carbs: 21.7g | Protein: 15.7g

INGREDIENTS

- 450g crescent rolls dough
- 2 eggs, whisked
- 500g cheddar cheese, grated
- 1 tbsp parmesan, grated
- 450g ham, cooked and chopped
- Salt and black pepper to the taste
- Cooking spray

DIRECTIONS

1. Spray the bottom of the air fryer pan with cooking spray, then press half of the crescent roll dough on it.
2. Whisk the eggs with the cheddar cheese, parmesan, salt, and pepper in a bowl before adding them to the dough.
3. Ham should be spread out, the remaining crescent roll dough should be cut into strips, placed over the ham, and baked for 25 minutes at 150°C.

Breakfast Veggie Mix

Prep Time: 10 Min | Cook Time: 25 Min | Serves: 6

Calories: 230.5 | Fat: 5.1g | Carbs: 20.3g | Protein: 11.8g

INGREDIENTS

- 1 yellow onion, sliced
- 1 red bell pepper, chopped
- 1 gold potato, chopped
- 2 tbsp olive oil
- 225g brie, trimmed and cubed
- 340g sourdough bread, cubed
- 100g parmesan, grated
- 8 eggs
- 2 tbsp mustard
- 750ml milk
- Salt and black pepper to the taste

DIRECTIONS

1. Your air fryer should be heated to 175°C before adding oil, onion, potato, and bell pepper and cooking for 5 minutes.
2. Whisk the eggs, milk, salt, pepper, and mustard together in a bowl.
3. Your air fryer should now include bread, brie, half the egg mixture, and half the parmesan.
4. Cook for 20 minutes before adding the remaining bread and parmesan and giving everything a quick stir. Serve and enjoy!

LUNCH RECIPES

Egg Rolls

Prep Time: 10 Min | Cook Time: 15 Min | Serves: 4

Calories: 170.3 | Fat: 6.1g | Carbs: 7.3g | Protein: 8.1g

INGREDIENTS

- 125g mushrooms, chopped
- 125g carrots, grated
- 125g zucchini, grated
- 2 green onions, chopped
- 2 tbsp soy sauce
- 8 egg roll wrappers
- 1 eggs, whisked
- 1 tbsp cornstarch

DIRECTIONS

1. Carrots should be thoroughly combined with mushrooms, zucchini, green onions, and soy sauce in a bowl.
2. Place egg roll wrappers on a work surface, divide the veggie mixture among them, and tightly roll each one.
3. Egg rolls should be brushed with a mixture of cornstarch and egg that has been thoroughly whisked.
4. Place all rolls in your warmed air fryer, seal the edges, and cook for 15 minutes at 185°C.

Stuffed Mushrooms

Prep Time: 10 Min | Cook Time: 20 Min | Serves: 4

Calories: 151.4 | Fat: 4.1g | Carbs: 8.3g | Protein: 5.1g

INGREDIENTS

- 4 big Portobello mushroom caps
- 1 tbsp olive oil
- 65g ricotta cheese
- 5 tbsp parmesan, grated
- 250g spinach, torn
- 60g bread crumbs
- ¼ tsp rosemary, chopped

DIRECTIONS

1. Mushroom caps should be rubbed with oil, put in the basket of your air fryer, and cooked for two minutes at 175°C.
2. In the meantime, combine the ricotta, spinach, rosemary, and bread crumbs in a bowl with half of the parmesan. Stir thoroughly.
3. Place the mushrooms in the basket of your air fryer once again, stuff them with this mixture, and then cook them at 175°C for 10 minutes.

Quick Lunch Pizzas

Prep Time: 10 Min | Cook Time: 7 Min | Serves: 4

Calories: 198.7 | Fat: 4.1g | Carbs: 7.5g | Protein: 3.1g

INGREDIENTS

- 4 pitas
- 1 tbsp olive oil
- 200ml pizza sauce
- 100g jarred mushrooms, sliced
- ½ tsp basil, dried
- 2 green onions, chopped
- 450g mozzarella, grated
- 250g grape tomatoes, sliced

DIRECTIONS

1. Spread pizza sauce on each pita bread, sprinkle green onions and basil, divide mushrooms and top with cheese.
2. Place pita pizzas in your air fryer and cook them for 7 minutes at 200°C.
3. Slices of tomato are added to each pizza.
4. Serve and enjoy!

Tuna and Zucchini Tortillas

Prep Time: 10 Min | Cook Time: 10 Min | Serves: 4

Calories: 162.4 | Fat: 4.1g | Carbs: 8.5g | Protein: 4.3g

INGREDIENTS

- 4 corn tortillas
- 4 tbsp butter, soft
- 170g canned tuna, drained
- 250g zucchini, shredded
- 60ml mayonnaise
- 2 tbsp mustard
- 250g cheddar cheese, grated

DIRECTIONS

1. Spread tortillas with butter, put them in the basket of your air fryer, and cook them for three minutes at 200°C.
2. In the meantime, combine the tuna, zucchini, mayo, and mustard in a bowl and toss.
3. Place a portion of this mixture on each tortilla, cover with cheese, roll the tortillas up, put them back in the basket of your air fryer, and cook them at 200°C for an additional 4 minutes.

Squash Fritters

Prep Time: 10 Min | Cook Time: 7 Min | Serves: 4

Calories: 200.5 | Fat: 4.2g | Carbs: 8.0g | Protein: 6.3g

INGREDIENTS

- 85g cream cheese
- 1 egg, whisked
- ½ tsp oregano, dried
- A pinch of salt and black pepper
- 1 yellow summer squash, grated
- 125g carrot, grated
- 125g bread crumbs
- 2 tbsp olive oil

DIRECTIONS

1. Salt, pepper, oregano, egg, breadcrumbs, carrots, and squash should all be combined with cream cheese in a bowl.
2. From this mixture, form medium patties and brush them with oil.
3. Squash patties should be placed in your air fryer and cooked for 7 minutes at 200°C.

Lunch Gnocchi

Prep Time: 10 Min | Cook Time: 17 Min | Serves: 4

Calories: 199.2 | Fat: 4.1g | Carbs: 11.5g | Protein: 4.1g

INGREDIENTS

- 1 yellow onion, chopped
- 1 tbsp olive oil
- 3 garlic cloves, minced
- 450g gnocchi
- 60g parmesan, grated
- 220g spinach pesto

DIRECTIONS

1. In your air fryer, coat the pan with olive oil, add the gnocchi, onion, and garlic, toss to combine, and cook for 10 minutes at 200°C.
2. At 175°C, add the pesto, mix, and cook for an additional 7 minutes.
3. Serve and enjoy!

Shrimp Croquettes

Prep Time: 10 Min | Cook Time: 8 Min | Serves: 4

Calories: 140.5 | Fat: 4.1g | Carbs: 9.0g | Protein: 4.2g

INGREDIENTS

- 400g shrimp, cooked, peeled, deveined and chopped
- 350g bread crumbs
- 1 egg, whisked
- 2 tbsp lemon juice
- 3 green onions, chopped
- ½ tsp basil, dried
- Salt and black pepper to the taste
- 2 tbsp olive oil

DIRECTIONS

1. Combine the egg, lemon juice, and half of the bread crumbs in a bowl and stir thoroughly.
2. Add the shrimp, basil, green onions, salt, and pepper, and stir thoroughly.
3. The remaining bread crumbs should be well combined with the oil in a different bowl.
4. Create spheres out of the shrimp mixture, roll them in bread crumbs, and cook them for 8 minutes at 200°C in an air fryer that has been warmed.
5. Serve and enjoy!

Chicken Sandwiches

Prep Time: 10 Min | Cook Time: 10 Min | Serves: 4

Calories: 125.5 | Fat: 4.1g | Carbs: 14.0g | Protein: 4.2g

INGREDIENTS

- 2 chicken breasts, skinless, boneless and cubed
- 1 red onion, chopped
- 1 red bell pepper, sliced
- 125ml Italian seasoning
- ½ tsp thyme, dried
- 450g butter lettuce, torn
- 4 pita pockets
- 250g cherry tomatoes, halved
- 1 tbsp olive oil

DIRECTIONS

1. Combine chicken with onion, bell pepper, Italian seasoning, and oil in an air fryer. Toss, then cook for 10 minutes at 195°C.
2. In a bowl, combine the chicken mixture with the thyme, butter lettuce, and cherry tomatoes. Fill the pita pockets with this mixture.
3. Serve and enjoy!

Fresh Chicken Mix

Prep Time: 10 Min | Cook Time: 20 Min | Serves: 4

Calories: 170.4 | Fat: 4.1g | Carbs: 12.0g | Protein: 4.1g

INGREDIENTS

- 2 chicken breasts, skinless, boneless and cubed
- 8 button mushrooms, sliced
- 1 red bell pepper, chopped
- 1 tbsp olive oil
- ½ tsp thyme, dried
- 280g Alfredo sauce
- 6 bread slices
- 2 tbsp butter, soft

DIRECTIONS

1. Combine the chicken, bell pepper, mushrooms, and oil in your air fryer, stir to thoroughly coat, and cook for 15 minutes at 175°C.
2. Transfer the chicken mixture to a bowl, top with the Alfredo sauce and thyme, and toss again. Cook at 175°C for an additional 4 minutes.
3. Spread butter on the bread slices, place them butter side up in the fryer, and cook for an additional 4 minutes.
4. Toast the bread slices, then place a chicken mixture on top of each.

Hot Bacon Sandwiches

Prep Time: 10 Min | Cook Time: 7 Min | Serves: 4

Calories: 182.1 | Fat: 6.0g | Carbs: 14.0g | Protein: 4.1g

INGREDIENTS

- 60ml BBQ sauce
- 2 tbsp honey
- 8 bacon slices, cooked and cut into thirds
- 1 red bell pepper, sliced
- 1 yellow bell pepper, sliced
- 3 pita pockets, halved
- 300g butter lettuce leaves, torn
- 2 tomatoes, sliced

DIRECTIONS

1. BBQ sauce and honey should be thoroughly combined in a bowl.
2. Place the bacon and all of the bell peppers in the air fryer and cook for 4 minutes at 175°C.
3. Shake the fryer and cook them a further 2 minutes.
4. Fill pita pockets with bacon mixture, tomatoes, and lettuce, and then top with the remaining barbecue sauce.

Buttermilk Chicken

Prep Time: 10 Min | Cook Time: 18 Min | Serves: 4

Calories: 199.3 | Fat: 3.0g | Carbs: 14.0g | Protein: 4.2g

INGREDIENTS

- 750g chicken thighs
- 450ml buttermilk
- Salt and black pepper to the taste
- A pinch of cayenne pepper
- 450g white flour
- 1 tbsp baking powder
- 1 tbsp sweet paprika
- 1 tbsp garlic powder

DIRECTIONS

1. Chicken thighs should be combined with buttermilk, salt, pepper, and cayenne in a bowl and then left to sit for six hours.
2. Stir together the flour, paprika, baking soda, and garlic powder in a separate bowl.
3. Place the drained chicken thighs in your air fryer and cook for 8 minutes at 180°C.
4. Flip the chicken pieces and cook them for an additional 10 minutes.

Chicken Pie

Prep Time: 10 Min | Cook Time: 15 Min | Serves: 4

Calories: 298.6 | Fat: 5.0g | Carbs: 14.0g | Protein: 7.2g

INGREDIENTS

- 2 chicken thighs, boneless, skinless and cubed
- 1 carrot, chopped
- 1 yellow onion, chopped
- 2 potatoes, chopped
- 2 mushrooms, chopped
- 1 tsp soy sauce
- Salt and black pepper to the taste
- 1 tsp Italian seasoning
- ½ tsp garlic powder
- 1 tsp Worcestershire sauce
- 1 tbsp flour
- 1 tbsp milk
- 2 puff pastry sheets
- 1 tbsp butter, melted

DIRECTIONS

1. In a pan, heat the oil over medium-high heat. When it is hot, add the potatoes, carrots, and onion. Stir for 2 minutes.
2. Stir thoroughly, then remove from heat after adding the milk, flour, chicken, soy sauce, pepper, Italian seasoning, garlic powder, and Worcestershire sauce.
3. Lay one puff pastry sheet on the pan of your air fryer and cut the excess pastry around the edges.
4. Add the chicken mixture, cover with the remaining puff pastry sheet, cut any excess, and butter the pie.
5. Put the food in your air fryer and cook for 6 minutes at 180°C.
6. Let pie cool before cutting and serving for lunch.

Mac and Cheese

Prep Time: 10 Min | Cook Time: 30 Min | Serves: 2

Calories: 339.6 | Fat: 7.0g | Carbs: 18.0g | Protein: 4.2g

INGREDIENTS

- 450g macaroni
- Cooking spray
- 125ml heavy cream
- 250ml chicken stock
- 200g cheddar cheese, shredded
- 125g mozzarella cheese, shredded
- 60g parmesan, shredded
- Salt and black pepper to the taste

DIRECTIONS

1. Spray a pan with cooking spray.
2. Add macaroni, heavy cream, stock, cheddar cheese, mozzarella and parmesan along with salt and pepper.
3. Stirring thoroughly, put pan in air fryer basket, and cook for 30 minutes.
4. Serve and enjoy!

Lunch Chicken Fajitas

Prep Time: 10 Min | Cook Time: 10 Min | Serves: 4

Calories: 315.2 | Fat: 6.0g | Carbs: 14.0g | Protein: 4.1g

INGREDIENTS

- 1 tsp garlic powder
- ¼ tsp cumin, ground
- ½ tsp chili powder
- Salt and black pepper to the taste
- ¼ tsp coriander, ground
- ½ kg chicken breasts, cut into strips
- 1 red bell pepper, sliced
- 1 green bell pepper, sliced
- 1 yellow onion, chopped
- 1 tbsp lime juice
- Cooking spray
- 4 tortillas, warmed up
- Salsa for serving
- Sour cream for serving
- 250g lettuce leaves, torn for serving

DIRECTIONS

1. Chicken should be combined with garlic powder, cumin, chili powder, salt, pepper, coriander, lime juice, green bell pepper, red bell pepper, and onion in a bowl. After 10 minutes, the mixture should be set aside. The chicken should then be transferred to your air fryer and covered with cooking spray.
2. Toss and cook for 10 minutes at 200°C.
3. Place tortillas on a work surface, divide the chicken mixture, and then top with salsa, sour cream, and lettuce. Wrap up, and you're ready to have lunch.

Fish And Chips

Prep Time: 10 Min | Cook Time: 12 Min | Serves: 2

Calories: 270.1 | Fat: 7.0g | Carbs: 14.0g | Protein: 4.0g

INGREDIENTS

- 2 medium cod fillets, skinless and boneless
- Salt and black pepper to the taste
- 60ml buttermilk
- 750g kettle chips, cooked

DIRECTIONS

1. Fish should be combined with buttermilk, salt, and pepper in a bowl and then set aside for five minutes.
2. Crush the chips in your food processor and spread them out on a platter.
3. Add the fish and firmly press it on both sides.
4. Transfer the fish to the basket of your air fryer, and cook for 12 minutes at 200°C.
5. Serve hot and enjoy!

Beef Cubes

Prep Time: 10 Min | Cook Time: 12 Min | Serves: 2

Calories: 269.8 | Fat: 6.0g | Carbs: 17.8g | Protein: 12.0g

INGREDIENTS

- ½ kg sirloin, cubed
- 450g jarred pasta sauce
- 450g bread crumbs
- 2 tbsp olive oil
- ½ tsp marjoram, dried
- White rice, already cooked for serving

DIRECTIONS

1. Beef chunks and pasta sauce should be combined well in a bowl.
2. Mix the bread crumbs, marjoram, and oil thoroughly in a separate bowl.
3. Beef cubes should be dipped in this mixture before being cooked at 180°C in an air fryer for 12 minutes.
4. Serve with white rice on the side after being divided among plates.

Pasta Salad

Prep Time: 10 Min | Cook Time: 12 Min | Serves: 6

Calories: 200.4 | Fat: 5.0g | Carbs: 9.8g | Protein: 6.0g

INGREDIENTS

- 1 zucchini, sliced in half and roughly chopped
- 1 orange bell pepper, roughly chopped
- 1 green bell pepper, roughly chopped
- 1 red onion, roughly chopped
- 100g brown mushrooms, halved
- Salt and black pepper to the taste
- 1 tsp Italian seasoning
- ½ kg penne rigate, already cooked
- 250g cherry tomatoes, halved
- 125g kalamata olive, pitted and halved
- 60ml olive oil
- 3 tbsp balsamic vinegar
- 2 tbsp basil, chopped

DIRECTIONS

1. Zucchini, mushrooms, red onion, orange and green bell peppers, salt, pepper, and Italian seasoning should all be combined in a bowl. The mixture should then be transferred to an air fryer that has been prepared to 195°C and cooked for 12 minutes.
2. Toss spaghetti with cooked vegetables, cherry tomatoes, olives, vinegar, and basil in a large salad bowl and serve for lunch.

Tasty Cheeseburgers

Prep Time: 10 Min | Cook Time: 20 Min | Serves: 2

Calories: 260.3 | Fat: 6.0g | Carbs: 19.8g | Protein: 6.1g

INGREDIENTS

- 340g lean beef, ground
- 4 tsp ketchup
- 3 tbsp yellow onion, chopped
- 2 tsp mustard
- Salt and black pepper to the taste
- 4 cheddar cheese slices
- 2 burger buns, halved

DIRECTIONS

1. Mix the meat, onion, ketchup, mustard, salt, and pepper in a bowl; stir well. Form the mixture into 4 patties.
2. Spread cheese over 2 patties, then add the remaining 2 patties on top.
3. Put them in an air fryer that has been preheated to 185°C and fried them for 20 minutes.
4. To assemble the cheeseburger for lunch, divide it among the two bun halves.

DINNER RECIPES

Herbed Chicken

Prep Time: 30 Min | Cook Time: 40 Min | Serves: 4

Calories: 388.4 | Fat: 10.0g | Carbs: 21.9g | Protein: 20.2g

INGREDIENTS

- 1 whole chicken
- Salt and black pepper to the taste
- 1 tsp garlic powder
- 1 tsp onion powder
- ½ tsp thyme, dried
- 1 tsp rosemary, dried
- 1 tbsp lemon juice
- 2 tbsp olive oil

DIRECTIONS

1. Rub the chicken with lemon juice and olive oil after seasoning it with salt and pepper, thyme, rosemary, garlic, and onion powder. Set the chicken aside for 30 minutes.
2. Place chicken in your air fryer and cook for 20 minutes on each side at 180°C.
3. Set aside the chicken to cool before carving and serving.

Rib Eye Steak

Prep Time: 10 Min | Cook Time: 20 Min | Serves: 4

Calories: 319.4 | Fat: 8.0g | Carbs: 21.9g | Protein: 20.1g

INGREDIENTS

- 1 kg rib eye steak
- Salt and black pepper to the taste
- 1 tbsp olive oil

For the rub:

- 3 tbsp sweet paprika
- 2 tbsp onion powder
- 2 tbsp garlic powder
- 1 tbsp brown sugar
- 2 tbsp oregano, dried
- 1 tbsp cumin, ground
- 1 tbsp rosemary, dried

DIRECTIONS

1. Stir together paprika, sugar, oregano, rosemary, salt, pepper, and cumin in a bowl. Use this mixture to season meat.
2. Rub the steak with salt and pepper, add it to the air fryer, and cook it for 20 minutes at 200°C, rotating it halfway through.
3. Place the steak on a cutting board, slice it, and add a side salad to the plate.

Delicious Catfish

Prep Time: 10 Min | Cook Time: 20 Min | Serves: 4

Calories: 252.3 | Fat: 6.0g | Carbs: 25.8g | Protein: 22.1g

INGREDIENTS

- 4 cat fish fillets
- Salt and black pepper to the taste
- A pinch of sweet paprika
- 1 tbsp parsley, chopped
- 1 tbsp lemon juice
- 1 tbsp olive oil

DIRECTIONS

1. Catfish fillets should be well-seasoned with salt, pepper, and paprika. They should then be placed in the basket of your air fryer and cooked for 20 minutes at 200°C, turning the fish over after 10 minutes.
2. Distribute the fish among the plates, top with lemon juice, garnish with parsley, and serve.

Soy Chicken Wings

Prep Time: 2 Hr | Cook Time: 15 Min | Serves: 6

Calories: 370.1 | Fat: 9.0g | Carbs: 36.9g | Protein: 23.2g

INGREDIENTS

- 16 chicken wings
- 2 tbsp honey
- 2 tbsp soy sauce
- Salt and black pepper to the taste
- ¼ tsp white pepper
- 3 tbsp lime juice

DIRECTIONS

1. In a bowl, combine honey, soy sauce, lime juice, salt, and black and white pepper; whisk well. Add the chicken pieces; toss to coat; and refrigerate for two hours.
2. Transfer the chicken to your air fryer and cook it for 3 more minutes at 200°C after cooking it at 185°C for 6 minutes on each side.
3. Serve hot.

Cod Fillets with Fennel and Grapes Salad

Prep Time: 10 Min | Cook Time: 15 Min | Serves: 2

Calories: 298.4 | Fat: 4.0g | Carbs: 31.8g | Protein: 22.2g

INGREDIENTS

- 2 black cod fillets, boneless
- 1 tbsp olive oil
- Salt and black pepper to the taste
- 1 fennel bulb, thinly sliced
- 250g grapes, halved
- 125g pecans

DIRECTIONS

1. Place fish fillets in the basket of your air fryer, drizzle half the oil over them, season with salt and pepper, rub well, and cook for 10 minutes at 200°C before transferring to a dish.
2. Toss pecans with grapes, fennel, the remaining oil, salt, and pepper in a bowl to combine. Transfer to a pan that fits your air fryer, and cook for 5 minutes at 200°C.
3. Distribute the fish among the plates and then serve with the fennel and grapes mixture.

Beef Strips with Snow Peas and Mushrooms

Prep Time: 10 Min | Cook Time: 22 Min | Serves: 2

Calories: 234.6 | Fat: 8.0g | Carbs: 21.9g | Protein: 24.1g

INGREDIENTS

- 2 beef steaks, cut into strips
- Salt and black pepper to the taste
- 200g snow peas
- 25g white mushrooms, halved
- 1 yellow onion, cut into rings
- 2 tbsp soy sauce
- 1 tsp olive oil

DIRECTIONS

1. Beef strips should be added to a bowl with the olive oil, soy sauce, and whisked mixture.
2. In a separate dish, combine the snow peas, onion, and mushrooms with the oil, salt, and pepper. Toss well, place the mixture in an air fryer-compatible pan, and cook for 16 minutes at 175°C.
3. Add beef strips to the pan and cook for an additional 6 minutes at 200°C.
4. Arrange the ingredients on plates and serve.

Creamy Coconut Chicken

Prep Time: 2 Hr | Cook Time: 25 Min | Serves: 4

Calories: 199.4 | Fat: 4.0g | Carbs: 21.9g | Protein: 20.2g

INGREDIENTS

- 4 big chicken legs
- 5 tsp turmeric powder
- 2 tbsp ginger, grated
- Salt and black pepper to the taste
- 4 tbsp coconut cream

DIRECTIONS

1. Mix the cream with the ginger, turmeric, salt, and pepper in a bowl.
2. Add the chicken pieces, combine them thoroughly, and set aside for two hours.
3. Transfer the chicken to your air fryer and prepare to 185°C.
4. Divide among plates and serve with a side salad after 25 minutes.

Steak and Broccoli

Prep Time: 45 Min | Cook Time: 12 Min | Serves: 4

Calories: 325.4 | Fat: 12.0g | Carbs: 22.9g | Protein: 23.1g

INGREDIENTS

- 500g round steak, cut into strips
- 350g broccoli florets
- 75ml oyster sauce
- 2 tsp sesame oil
- 1 tsp soy sauce
- 1 tsp sugar
- 75ml sherry
- 1 tbsp olive oil
- 1 garlic clove, minced

DIRECTIONS

1. Sesame oil, oyster sauce, soy sauce, sherry, and sugar should all be combined in a bowl along with the sugar. Add the meat, toss, and set away for 30 minutes.
2. Transfer the meat to a pan that will fit your air fryer. Add the broccoli, garlic, and oil as well. Toss everything together and cook for 12 minutes at 195°C.
3. Distribute among plates, and serve.

Chicken Parmesan

Prep Time: 10 Min | Cook Time: 15 Min | Serves: 4

Calories: 302.4 | Fat: 12.0g | Carbs: 21.9g | Protein: 15.2g

INGREDIENTS

- 450g panko bread crumbs
- 60g parmesan, grated
- ½ tsp garlic powder
- 450g white flour
- 1 egg, whisked
- 750g chicken cutlets, skinless and boneless
- Salt and black pepper to the taste
- 250g mozzarella, grated
- 450ml tomato sauce
- 3 tbsp basil, chopped

DIRECTIONS

1. Panko, parmesan, and garlic powder are combined in a bowl and stirred.
2. Add the egg to a third bowl and the flour to a second bowl.
3. Add salt and pepper to the chicken before dredging it in flour, then egg mixture, and finally panko.
4. Place the chicken pieces in your air fryer and cook them for 3 minutes on each side at 180°C.
5. Place the chicken in a baking dish that fits your air fryer, sprinkle with mozzarella and tomato sauce, and cook for 7 minutes at 190°C.
6. Distribute among plates, cover with basil, and serve.

Tabasco Shrimp

Prep Time: 10 Min | Cook Time: 10 Min | Serves: 4

Calories: 198.4 | Fat: 5.0g | Carbs: 12.8g | Protein: 8.2g

INGREDIENTS

- ½ kg shrimp, peeled and deveined
- 1 tsp red pepper flakes
- 2 tbsp olive oil
- 1 tsp Tabasco sauce
- 2 tbsp water
- 1 tsp oregano, dried
- Salt and black pepper to the taste
- ½ tsp parsley, dried
- ½ tsp smoked paprika

DIRECTIONS

1. Toss the shrimp in a bowl with the oil, water, Tabasco sauce, pepper flakes, oregano, parsley, salt, and pepper.
2. Add the shrimp to the 185°C preheated air fryer, and cook for 10 minutes while shaking the fryer.
3. Distribute the shrimp among the plates, along with a side salad.

Provencal Pork

Prep Time: 10 Min | Cook Time: 15 Min | Serves: 2

Calories: 299.4 | Fat: 8.0g | Carbs: 20.9g | Protein: 23.1g

INGREDIENTS

- 1 red onion, sliced
- 1 yellow bell pepper, cut into strips
- 1 green bell pepper, cut into strips
- Salt and black pepper to the taste
- 2 tsp Provencal herbs
- ½ tbsp mustard
- 1 tbsp olive oil
- 200g pork tenderloin

DIRECTIONS

1. Combine yellow and green bell peppers, onion, salt, pepper, Provencal herbs, and half the oil in a baking dish that will fit your air fryer and toss to combine.
2. Toss the pork with the remaining oil, salt, pepper, mustard, and vegetables.
3. Add everything to the air fryer, cook for 15 minutes at 185°C, then divide among plates and serve.

Mexican Chicken

Prep Time: 10 Min | Cook Time: 20 Min | Serves: 4

Calories: 339.4 | Fat: 18.0g | Carbs: 30.9g | Protein: 18.1g

INGREDIENTS

- 450ml salsa verde
- 1 tbsp olive oil
- Salt and black pepper to the taste
- ½ kg chicken breast, boneless and skinless
- 350g Monterey Jack cheese, grated
- 60g cilantro, chopped
- 1 tsp garlic powder

DIRECTIONS

1. Place salsa verde in a baking dish that will fit your air fryer, top with chicken that has been seasoned with salt, pepper, and garlic powder and brushed with olive oil.
2. Add the ingredients to your air fryer and cook for 20 minutes at 195°C.
3. Add cheese and cook for an additional 2 minutes.

Garlic Lamb Chops

Prep Time: 10 Min | Cook Time: 10 Min | Serves: 4

Calories: 230.6 | Fat: 7.0g | Carbs: 13.9g | Protein: 23.1g

INGREDIENTS

- 3 tbsp olive oil
- 8 lamb chops
- Salt and black pepper to the taste
- 4 garlic cloves, minced
- 1 tbsp oregano, chopped
- 1 tbsp coriander, chopped

DIRECTIONS

1. Lamb chops should be coated with oregano, salt, pepper, oil, garlic, and other seasonings.
2. Add the lamb chops to the air fryer and cook for 10 minutes at 200°C.
3. Distribute the lamb chops among plates and add a side salad.

Buttered Shrimp Skewers

Prep Time: 10 Min | Cook Time: 5 Min | Serves: 2

Calories: 139.4 | Fat: 1.0g | Carbs: 14.9g | Protein: 7.2g

INGREDIENTS

- 8 shrimps, peeled and deveined
- 4 garlic cloves, minced
- Salt and black pepper to the taste
- 8 green bell pepper slices
- 1 tbsp rosemary, chopped
- 1 tbsp butter, melted

DIRECTIONS

1. Shrimp, garlic, butter, salt, pepper, rosemary, and bell pepper slices should all be combined in a bowl. Toss to combine, then set aside for 10 minutes.
2. Skewer two shrimp and two slices of bell pepper. Repeat with the remaining shrimp and bell pepper pieces.
3. Put them all in the basket of your air fryer and cook for 6 minutes at 180°C.
4. Distribute across plates and serve immediately.

SNACKS RECIPES

Coconut Chicken Bites

Prep Time: 10 Min | Cook Time: 12 Min | Serves: 4

Calories: 250.4 | Fat: 4.0g | Carbs: 13.9g | Protein: 24.1g

INGREDIENTS

- 2 tsp garlic powder
- 2 eggs
- Salt and black pepper to the taste
- 175g panko bread crumbs
- 175g coconut, shredded
- Cooking spray
- 8 chicken tenders

DIRECTIONS

1. Eggs should be whisked together in a bowl with salt, pepper, and garlic powder.
2. Thoroughly combine coconut and panko in a separate bowl.
3. Coat chicken tenders with coconut oil after dipping them in egg mixture.
4. Cook chicken bits in the basket of your air fryer for 10 minutes at 175°Cahrenheit after spraying them with cooking spray.

Banana Snack

Prep Time: 10 Min | Cook Time: 5 Min | Serves: 8

Calories: 70.2 | Fat: 4.0g | Carbs: 9.9g | Protein: 1.1g

INGREDIENTS

- 16 baking cups crust
- 65g peanut butter
- 50g chocolate chips
- 1 banana, peeled and sliced into 16 pieces
- 1 tbsp vegetable oil

DIRECTIONS

1. Chocolate chips should be heated in a small pot over low heat, stirred until melted, then the heat should be turned off.
2. Combine peanut butter and coconut oil in a bowl and whisk to combine.
3. Place 1 banana slice and 1 tsp butter mixture in a cup, then top with 1 tsp chocolate mixture.
4. Repeat with the remaining cups, put them all in an air fryer-compatible dish, cook at 160°Cahrenheit for 5 minutes, then move to a freezer and keep there until you're ready to serve them as a snack.

Buffalo Cauliflower Bites

Prep Time: 10 Min | Cook Time: 15 Min | Serves: 4

Calories: 240.2 | Fat: 4.0g | Carbs: 7.9g | Protein: 4.1g

INGREDIENTS

- 900g cauliflower florets
- 250g panko bread crumbs
- 60g butter, melted
- 65ml buffalo sauce
- Mayonnaise for serving

DIRECTIONS

1. Whisk butter and buffalo sauce together in a bowl.
2. Coat panko bread crumbs on cauliflower florets after dipping them in this mixture.
3. Put them in the basket of your air fryer and cook for 15 minutes at 175°C.
4. Put them on a dish and provide mayo on the side.

Shrimp Muffins

Prep Time: 10 Min | Cook Time: 25 Min | Serves: 5

Calories: 60.2 | Fat: 2.0g | Carbs: 4.1g | Protein: 4.0g

INGREDIENTS

- 1 spaghetti squash, peeled and halved
- 2 tbsp mayonnaise
- 250g mozzarella, shredded
- 225g shrimp, peeled, cooked and chopped
- 350g panko
- 1 tsp parsley flakes
- 1 garlic clove, minced
- Salt and black pepper to the taste
- Cooking spray

DIRECTIONS

1. Squash halves should be placed in your air fryer, heated to 175°C or 16 minutes, then set aside to cool so that the flesh can be scraped into a bowl.
2. Stir thoroughly after adding the salt, pepper, parsley flakes, panko, shrimp, mayo, and mozzarella.
3. Use cooking spray to coat a muffin pan that fits your air fryer, then divide the squash and shrimp mixture among the cups.
4. Add the food to the fryer and cook for 10 minutes at 180°C.
5. Serve muffins on a tray as a snack.

Zucchini Cakes

Prep Time: 10 Min | Cook Time: 12 Min | Serves: 12

Calories: 60.2 | Fat: 2.0g | Carbs: 6.1g | Protein: 2.0g

INGREDIENTS

- Cooking spray
- 120g dill, chopped
- 1 egg
- 125g whole wheat flour
- Salt and black pepper to the taste
- 1 yellow onion, chopped
- 2 garlic cloves, minced
- 3 zucchinis, grated

DIRECTIONS

1. Combine the zucchinis with the garlic, onion, flour, salt, pepper, egg, and dill in a bowl.
2. Stir well. Form small patties from this mixture.
3. Place them in the basket of your air fryer.
4. Cook for 6 minutes on each side at 185°C.
5. Serve and enjoy!

Cauliflower Bars

Prep Time: 10 Min | Cook Time: 25 Min | Serves: 12

Calories: 50.1 | Fat: 1.0g | Carbs: 3.1g | Protein: 3.0g

INGREDIENTS

- 1 big cauliflower head, florets separated
- 125g mozzarella, shredded
- 60ml egg whites
- 1 tsp Italian seasoning
- Salt and black pepper to the taste

DIRECTIONS

1. Cauliflower florets should be placed in a food processor, pulsed well, spread out on a prepared baking sheet that is the right size for your air fryer, put in the fryer, and cooked for 10 minutes at 180°C.
2. Place the cauliflower in a bowl, season with salt, pepper, cheese, egg whites, and Italian seasoning, and stir vigorously. Spread the mixture into a rectangular pan that will fit your air fryer, press it down firmly, place it inside, and cook at 180°C for an additional 15 minutes.
3. Slice the recipe into 12 bars, place them on a plate, and serve as a snack.

Mexican Apple Snack

Prep Time: 10 Min | Cook Time: 5 Min | Serves: 4

Calories: 199.2 | Fat: 4.0g | Carbs: 20.1g | Protein: 3.0g

INGREDIENTS

- 3 big apples, cored, peeled and cubed
- 2 tsp lemon juice
- 60g pecans, chopped
- 120g dark chocolate chips
- 125ml caramel sauce

DIRECTIONS

1. Apples and lemon juice should be combined in a bowl, stirred, and then placed in an air fryer-compatible pan.
2. Add the ingredients to the air fryer and mix to combine. Cook for 5 minutes at 160°C. Add the chocolate chips and pecans. Drizzle with the caramel sauce.
3. Gently toss, divide into small bowls, and serve as a snack immediately away.

Salmon Party Patties

Prep Time: 10 Min | Cook Time: 22 Min | Serves: 4

Calories: 230.4 | Fat: 3.0g | Carbs: 14.1g | Protein: 4.0g

INGREDIENTS

- 3 big potatoes, boiled, drained and mashed
- 1 big salmon fillet, skinless, boneless
- 2 tbsp parsley, chopped
- 2 tbsp dill, chopped
- Salt and black pepper to the taste
- 1 egg
- 2 tbsp bread crumbs
- Cooking spray

DIRECTIONS

1. Salmon should be placed in the basket of your air fryer and cooked for 10 minutes at 180°C.
2. Place the salmon on a chopping board, let it cool, then flake it into a bowl.
3. Stir in the mashed potatoes, salt, pepper, dill, parsley, egg, and bread crumbs before forming the mixture into 8 patties.
4. Put the salmon patties in the basket of your air fryer, coat them with cooking oil, and cook them for 12 minutes at 180°C while flipping them halfway through. Then, transfer them to a tray and serve as an appetizer.

Pumpkin Muffins

Prep Time: 10 Min | Cook Time: 15 Min | Serves: 18

Calories: 50.1 | Fat: 3.0g | Carbs: 2.1g | Protein: 2.0g

INGREDIENTS

- 125g butter
- 150ml pumpkin puree
- 2 tbsp flaxseed meal
- 60g flour
- 125g sugar
- ½ tsp nutmeg, ground
- 1 tsp cinnamon powder
- ½ tsp baking soda
- 1 egg
- ½ tsp baking powder

DIRECTIONS

1. Butter, pumpkin puree, and egg are thoroughly combined in a bowl.
2. Stir well after adding the flaxseed meal, flour, sugar, baking soda, baking powder, nutmeg, and cinnamon.
3. Spoon this mixture into a muffin tin that will fit your fryer. Bake for 15 minutes at 175°C.
4. Serve muffins as a cold snack.

Beef Jerky Snack

Prep Time: 2 Hr | Cook Time: 1 Hr 30 Min | Serves: 6

Calories: 50.1 | Fat: 3.0g | Carbs: 2.1g | Protein: 2.0g

INGREDIENTS

- 450ml soy sauce
- 125ml Worcestershire sauce
- 2 tbsp black peppercorns
- 2 tbsp black pepper
- 1 kg beef round, sliced

DIRECTIONS

1. Blend the soy sauce, Worcestershire sauce, black pepper, and black peppercorns together in a bowl.
2. Add the beef slices, stir to coat, and set aside for 6 hours in the refrigerator.
3. Place beef rounds in your air fryer and cook them for 1 hour and 30 minutes at 185°C.
4. Move to a bowl, then serve chilled.

Honey Party Wings

Prep Time: 1 Hr 10 Min | Cook Time: 12 Min | Serves: 8

Calories: 210.3 | Fat: 4.0g | Carbs: 14.2g | Protein: 3.0g

INGREDIENTS

- 16 chicken wings, halved
- 2 tbsp soy sauce
- 2 tbsp honey
- Salt and black pepper to the taste
- 2 tbsp lime juice

DIRECTIONS

1. Chicken wings should be combined with soy sauce, honey, salt, pepper, and lime juice in a bowl. Stir well, and then chill for an hour.
2. Place the chicken wings in the air fryer, flip them halfway through cooking for 12 minutes at 180°C.
3. Put them in a serving plate and offer them as an appetizer.

DESSERT RECIPES

Banana Cake

Prep Time: 10 Min | Cook Time: 30 Min | Serves: 4

Calories: 231.4 | Fat: 4.0g | Carbs: 34.1g | Protein: 4.0g

INGREDIENTS

- 1 tbsp butter, soft
- 1 egg
- 150g brown sugar
- 2 tbsp honey
- 1 banana, peeled and mashed
- 250g white flour
- 1 tsp baking powder
- ½ tsp cinnamon powder
- Cooking spray

DIRECTIONS

1. Cooking spray should be used to coat a cake pan, then set it aside.
2. In a bowl, combine together the butter, sugar, honey, banana, egg, cinnamon, baking powder, and flour.
3. Pour this mixture into a cake pan that has been greased with cooking spray, add it to your air fryer, and cook for 30 minutes at 175°C.
4. Let the cake cool before slicing and serving.

Bread Pudding

Prep Time: 10 Min | Cook Time: 1 Hr | Serves: 4

Calories: 301.4 | Fat: 8.0g | Carbs: 23.1g | Protein: 10.0g

INGREDIENTS

- 6 glazed doughnuts, crumbled
- 250g cherries
- 4 egg yolks
- 350ml whipping cream
- 125g raisins
- 60g sugar
- 60g chocolate chips

DIRECTIONS

1. Cherries, egg yolks, and whipping cream are well combined in a bowl.
2. Stir together raisins, sugar, chocolate chips, and doughnuts in a separate bowl.
3. Combine the two mixtures, transfer the contents to a pan that fits your air fryer, and bake the food for an hour at 150°C.
4. Chill before slicing and serving the pudding.

Cocoa Cake

Prep Time: 10 Min | Cook Time: 15 Min | Serves: 6

Calories: 339.5 | Fat: 11.0g | Carbs: 25.1g | Protein: 5.0g

INGREDIENTS

- 100g pumpkin flesh, chopped
- 3 eggs
- 75g sugar
- 1 tsp cocoa powder
- 85g flour
- ½ tsp lemon juice

DIRECTIONS

1. Whisk 1 tbsp of butter into the cocoa powder in a bowl.
2. In another bowl, whisk together the remaining butter, sugar, eggs, flour, and lemon juice. Pour half of the mixture into an air fryer-compatible cake pan.
3. Spread the first half of the cocoa mixture on top, then add the remaining butter layer and finish with the remaining cocoa.
4. Add the ingredients to your air fryer and cook for 17 minutes at 180°C.
5. Let cake cool completely before cutting and serving.

Pumpkin Pie

Prep Time: 10 Min | Cook Time: 15 Min | Serves: 9

Calories: 199.4 | Fat: 5.0g | Carbs: 5.1g | Protein: 6.0g

INGREDIENTS

- 1 tbsp sugar
- 2 tbsp flour
- 1 tbsp butter
- 2 tbsp water

For the pumpkin pie filling:

- 100g pumpkin flesh, chopped
- 1 tsp mixed spice
- 1 tsp nutmeg
- 85ml water
- 1 egg, whisked
- 1 tbsp sugar

DIRECTIONS

1. Using an immersion blender, blend the mixture after turning off the heat. Place 85ml of water in a pot, add it to a boil over medium-high heat, and then add pumpkin, an egg, 1 tbsp of sugar, spice, and nutmeg.
2. Prepare your dough by combining flour, butter, 1 tbsp of sugar, and 2 tbsp of water in a bowl.
3. Butter a pie pan that fits your air fryer, press dough into the pan, fill with pumpkin pie filling, put in the basket of your air fryer, and cook for 15 minutes at 180°C.
4. Slice and serve warm.

Apple Bread

Prep Time: 10 Min | Cook Time: 40 Min | Serves: 6

Calories: 190.2 | Fat: 6.0g | Carbs: 14.1g | Protein: 7.0g

INGREDIENTS

- 600g apples, cored and cubed
- 250g sugar
- 1 tbsp vanilla
- 2 eggs
- 1 tbsp apple pie spice
- 500g white flour
- 1 tbsp baking powder
- 1 stick butter
- 250ml water

DIRECTIONS

1. Use your mixer to combine the egg, sugar, apple pie spice, and 1 butter stick in a bowl.
2. Add the apples and stir thoroughly once more.
3. Stir baking powder into flour in a separate dish.
4. Mix the two mixes together, then pour the mixture into a springform pan.
5. Cook a springform pan in your air fryer for 40 minutes at 160°Cahrenheit.
6. Slice and serve.

Ginger Cheesecake

Prep Time: 2 Hr 10 Min | Cook Time: 20 Min | Serves: 6

Calories: 408.2 | Fat: 12.0g | Carbs: 20.1g | Protein: 6.0g

INGREDIENTS

- 2 tsp butter, melted
- 125g ginger cookies, crumbled
- 450g cream cheese, soft
- 2 eggs
- 125g sugar
- 1 tsp rum
- ½ tsp vanilla extract
- ½ tsp nutmeg, ground

DIRECTIONS

1. Spread cookie crumbs on the bottom of a pan that has been greased with butter.
2. Spread cream cheese over the cookie crumbs after thoroughly mixing it with eggs, nutmeg, vanilla, and rum.
3. Add the ingredients to your air fryer and cook for 20 minutes at 170°C.
4. Before slicing and serving cheesecake, allow it to cool and chill in the refrigerator for two hours.

Cocoa Cookies

Prep Time: 10 Min | Cook Time: 15 Min | Serves: 12

Calories: 178.2 | Fat: 14.0g | Carbs: 3.1g | Protein: 5.0g

INGREDIENTS

- 150ml coconut oil, melted
- 6 eggs
- 85g cocoa powder
- 2 tsp vanilla
- ½ tsp baking powder
- 100g cream cheese
- 5 tbsp sugar

DIRECTIONS

1. Blend eggs with coconut oil, swerve, cream cheese, cocoa powder, baking soda, and vanilla in a blender.
2. Place this in an air fryer-compatible lined baking dish, preheat to 160°C, and bake for 14 minutes.
3. Cut the rectangles from the cookie sheet and serve.

Special Walnuts Brownies

Prep Time: 10 Min | Cook Time: 17 Min | Serves: 4

Calories: 221.2 | Fat: 32.0g | Carbs: 3.1g | Protein: 6.0g

INGREDIENTS

- 1 egg
- 150g cocoa powder
- 150g sugar
- 7 tbsp butter
- ½ tsp vanilla extract
- 75g white flour
- 60g walnuts, chopped
- ½ tsp baking powder
- 1 tbsp peanut butter

DIRECTIONS

1. A pan should be heated with 6 tbsp of butter and the sugar. Stirring frequently, cook for 5 minutes, remove from heat, transfer to a bowl, add salt, vanilla extract, cocoa powder, egg, baking powder, walnuts, and flour, thoroughly stir everything together, and then pour into a pan that fits your air fryer.
2. Combine 1 tbsp butter and 1 tbsp peanut butter in a bowl, microwave for a brief period of time, stir well, and then pour this over the brownie batter.
3. Add the ingredients to your air fryer and bake for 17 minutes at 160°Cahrenheit.
4. After the brownies have cooled, slice them and serve.

Bread Dough Amaretto Dessert

Prep Time: 10 Min | Cook Time: 12 Min | Serves: 12

Calories: 301.4 | Fat: 8.0g | Carbs: 23.1g | Protein: 10.0g

INGREDIENTS

- ½ kg bread dough
- 250g sugar
- 125g butter, melted
- 250ml heavy cream
- 340g chocolate chips
- 2 tbsp amaretto liqueur

DIRECTIONS

1. The dough is rolled, cut into 20 slices, and then each piece is sliced in half.
2. Place the dough pieces in your air fryer's basket after brushing the basket with butter. Cook the dough pieces at 175°C for 5 minutes, flip them over, cook for another 3 minutes, and then transfer them to a platter.
3. Melt the chocolate chips by adding them to a pan with heavy cream that has been heated over medium heat.
4. Add the liquor, whisk once more, transfer to a bowl, and serve the sauce with the bread dippers.

Blueberry Scones

Prep Time: 10 Min | Cook Time: 10 Min | Serves: 10

Calories: 129.2 | Fat: 2.0g | Carbs: 4.1g | Protein: 3.0g

INGREDIENTS

- 250g white flour
- 200g blueberries
- 2 eggs
- 125ml heavy cream
- 125g butter
- 5 tbsp sugar
- 2 tsp vanilla extract
- 2 tsp baking powder

DIRECTIONS

1. Flour, salt, baking powder, and blueberries are combined in a bowl and stirred.
2. Combine heavy cream, butter, sugar, eggs, and vanilla extract in a separate bowl.
3. Combine the two mixtures, knead the dough until it forms 10 triangles, lay the triangles on a lined baking sheet that fits your air fryer, and cook the triangles for 10 minutes at 160°C.
4. Serve them cold.

Choco Cookies

Prep Time: 10 Min | Cook Time: 25 Min | Serves: 12

Calories: 230.2 | Fat: 12.0g | Carbs: 4.1g | Protein: 5.0g

INGREDIENTS

- 1 tsp vanilla extract
- 125g butter
- 1 egg
- 4 tbsp sugar
- 450g flour
- 125g unsweetened chocolate chips

DIRECTIONS

1. Butter should be heated in a skillet over medium heat, stirred, and cooked for one minute.
2. Combine the egg, sugar, and vanilla essence in a bowl and stir thoroughly.
3. Stir in the flour, melted butter, and half of the chocolate chips.
4. Place mixture in a pan that will fit your air fryer, cover with the remaining chocolate chips, and bake for 25 minutes at 165°C.
5. When it is cold, slice and serve.

Orange Cake

Prep Time: 10 Min | Cook Time: 32 Min | Serves: 12

Calories: 200.2 | Fat: 13.0g | Carbs: 9.1g | Protein: 8.0g

INGREDIENTS

- 6 eggs
- 1 orange, peeled and cut into quarters
- 1 tsp vanilla extract
- 1 tsp baking powder
- 250g flour
- 50g sugar+ 2 tbsp
- 2 tbsp orange zest
- 100g cream cheese
- 100g yogurt

DIRECTIONS

1. Orange should be well pulsed in your food processor.
2. Continue to pulse before adding the flour, 2 tbsp of sugar, eggs, baking powder, and vanilla essence.
3. Place each of these in your fryer and cook them at 165°C for 16 minutes.
4. In the meantime, thoroughly combine the cream cheese, yogurt, and remaining sugar in a bowl.
5. To assemble the cake, place one layer on a plate, top with half of the cream cheese mixture, then add the second layer and finish with the remaining cream cheese mixture.
6. Evenly spread it, cut it, and serve.

Printed in Great Britain
by Amazon

16299873R00052